THE LITTLE BOOK OF

big
ideas

ABOUT

Spirituality

ed J. pinegar

EAGLE
GATE

Library of Congress Catalog Card Number 00-133332

ISBN 1-57345-828-7

Printed in Mexico   18961-6723

10   9   8   7   6   5   4   3   2   1

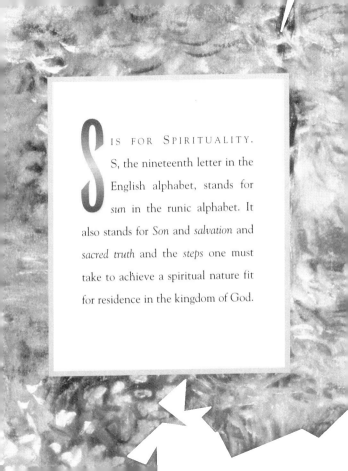

S IS FOR SPIRITUALITY.
S, the nineteenth letter in the English alphabet, stands for *sun* in the runic alphabet. It also stands for *Son* and *salvation* and *sacred truth* and the *steps* one must take to achieve a spiritual nature fit for residence in the kingdom of God.

Next time you have a chance to read whatever you choose, consider taking a look at a reference book that reviews the development of the alphabet. It is fascinating! The stunning fact of it, to me, however, is the dilemma clearly presented by the idea of how change comes about, how error creeps into truth, and how people are subsequently led astray. Then think about this: Over the generations, variation has evolved not only in language and alphabets, but also in the perception of God and worship, values and standards of behavior, good and evil, the purpose of life, and the way to get to heaven.

What happens if one has not engaged in a prayerful study of the ultimate knowledge in life? Or if such a wholesome, sincere search has been limited to the changed doctrine with which many religions have been left after history's verified apostasy and reformation? Life simply won't be what God wants for us, either now or in eternity. Surely there is wisdom in searching the depths of restored truth and studying the power of God in our day regarding these compelling aspects of life, death, and joy.

Even though thousands are finding truth, too many have settled for less. This collection of ideas is a quick yet profound read on revealed truth. Each page contains a nugget of truth about the necessary steps in achieving true spirituality. I have collected these treasures from the writings of Dr. Ed J. Pinegar, popular teacher, scholar, and priesthood leader, whose joy-bringing ideas about spirituality will enrich your life.

Elaine Cannon

Spirituality is the goal of those who yearn to be Christlike and truly seek the will of God as a *priority*, not just as a passing statement or a New Year's resolution.

The Lord expects us to succeed in becoming even as he is (3 Nephi 27:27). He will guide us every step of the way if we'll allow it.

HOW DOES REAL SPIRITUALITY COME ABOUT?

WHAT ARE THE STEPS ONE TAKES TO MAKE THIS

ADJUSTMENT IN LIFE? BASED ON THE WORDS OF

ANCIENT AND MODERN PROPHETS, CONSIDER THE

FOLLOWING STEPS TO GREATER SPIRITUALITY.

THE TWELVE STEPS ARE:

1. *Remembrance*

2. *Love*

3. *Humility*

4. *Teachableness*

5. *Understanding the Atonement*

6. *Gratitude*

7. *A desire to do good*

8. *Faith*

9. *Charity*

10. *Obedience*

11. *Self-mastery*

12. *Endurance*

STEP ONE:

REMEMBRANCE

Recognize and remember God's
goodness, mercy, covenants, his sacred
promises to us, and his love for us.

When we remember the goodness of God, our love for God increases; then we depend on God in all things and reach a new state of humility. As we continue to press forward with a heart open to further teaching, we learn to apply each gospel principle to our lives, which helps us endure to the end. We yearn to someday return to heaven and be in the presence of our Heavenly Father because we love him.

STEP TWO:
LOVE

Love of God floods our soul in an incredible reality of heavenly affection. This results in a state of awe before him, and we are humbled! We are converted! We want to love as God loves and live as he has commanded us.

When we are converted, it is a kindness to share truth and goodness with others in order to strengthen their faith. This word of God is the secret of lasting love: "Thou shalt love the Lord thy God with all thy heart, and with all thy soul, and with all thy mind. This is the first and great commandment. And the second is like unto it, Thou shalt love thy neighbour as thyself" (MATTHEW 22:37–39).

STEP THREE:

HUMILITY

In a submissive and receptive state of
humility, our understanding is quickened
because of our relationship to God.

When we are humbled we sense our dependency upon our Heavenly Father for direction through the realms of life here and hereafter. We become independent of the world, willing to be easily entreated and more teachable.

STEP FOUR:
TEACHABLENESS

Converted people are different people. They act differently. They have no more desire to do evil. They are happy. They are grateful, feeling indebted to the Lord their God for their eternal lives. They want to know more of truth and more about the will of God.

BEING TEACHABLE IS A CONTAGIOUS AND GOOD THING! ONE PERSON BEING WILLING TO LISTEN, TO LEARN, TO CONSIDER, AND TO WEIGH A THOUGHT SETS A PLEASANT EXAMPLE FOR OTHERS IN A CLASSROOM OR FAMILY SETTING. IT IS INSPIRING TO OTHERS TO ACCEPT TRUTH, TO GROW AND MOVE TOWARD A HIGHER GOAL.

If we don't know his will we can't really live it, now can we? Maybe by accident but not by conscious choice, which is what our agency is about. The blessings of the Lord depend on our willingness to be taught.

Joseph F. Smith said: "I cannot save you; you cannot save me; we cannot save each other, only so far as we can persuade each other to receive the truth, by teaching it. When a man receives the truth he will be saved by it. He will not be saved merely because someone talked to him, but because he received and acted upon it." These are tremendously important words. Think about them.

UNDERSTANDING THE ATONEMENT

This gift is so vital to everything else in our lives that we need to study the fact of it. Understanding and appreciating the doctrine of the Atonement is the key to change and progression. It is rooted in our Savior Jesus Christ, so our learning begins with a study of him.

The Atonement is more than just an essential part of coming unto Christ; it is absolutely imperative. Jesus himself said: "No man taketh [my life] from me, but I lay it down of myself. I have the power to lay it down, and I have the power to take it again" (JOHN 10:18).

Being the divine Son of God, one who had himself raised the dead, Jesus could have saved himself on the cross. Yet he *gave* his life for us that everyone would be resurrected at some time beyond this life.

As we ponder what that unselfish act of Jesus Christ meant, as we consider the plight of mankind in his fallen state, a wonderful feeling begins to well up inside our souls. We feel gratitude.

GRATITUDE

Gratitude is a realization of God's incredible
kindness. It is the seed of all righteous
desires. It is a by-product of purposeful
God-centered living. Gratitude—a truly
cardinal virtue—is the catalyst that brings
all the steps of spirituality together.

Gratitude precipitates growth and
change. Gratitude is the link
between the person who understands
the magnificent Atonement and
draws closer to Christ as a disciple.

CONVERTS OFTEN SAY THAT FOLLOWING THEIR

CONVERSION THEY CAN HARDLY WAIT TO PAY

BACK THEIR DEBTS FOR ALL OF GOD'S GOODNESS.

THEIR BELIEF IS THE ESSENCE OF GOOD ACTION.

When asked about his conversion, the

great composer Stravinsky said he

studied the Gospels. He wanted to know

what Jesus said, not a denominational

interpretation. He composed music that

would bring people closer to God.

A DESIRE TO DO GOOD

When we are converted, we become
responsible and accountable individuals
recognizing the worth of all souls and
desiring to help others.

WHEN THE SPIRIT IS UPON US, WE DESIRE TO

TEACH, PREACH, BLESS, AND SERVE MANKIND.

WE BEGIN TO CHOOSE GOALS AND FOLLOW A LIFE

CONGRUENT WITH THE GOSPEL OF JESUS CHRIST

AND TO HELP OTHERS SEE LIFE IN THIS LIGHT.

In my role as a mission president in England, I had a tender interview with a young missionary who wanted to go home. I asked him how he felt about his Heavenly Father and the Lord. He was frustrated and didn't fully understand his relationship with God or the many blessings he had received at God's hand. We talked of God's goodness and tender mercy. We rehearsed how much he had done for us and how we should thank him by loving and serving him.

As the missionary caught hold of the meaning of some of these words, the Spirit touched his heart. We discussed

the love of God and the infinite
atonement of Christ. The idea of the
Atonement began to make an impact
on his heart and mind as he learned
things he had not before known or
felt. And at last we cried together
and he cried out, "Oh, President. . . .
I want to stay. I love the Lord. I want
to help."

The great prophet Jacob explained
this change: "And we did magnify our
office unto the Lord, taking upon us
the responsibility, answering the sins
of the people upon our own heads if
we did not teach them the word of
God with all diligence" (JACOB 1:19).

STEP EIGHT:

FAITH

Faith is the first principle of the

gospel of Jesus in its purity

because upon it all else stands.

FAITH IS CALMING. FAITH ERASES FEAR. FAITH

LIFTS THE SPIRIT AND FILLS THE HEART WITH

HOPE NO MATTER WHAT GOES ON OUTSIDE US.

THE PRICE WE PAY FOR FAITH IS FASTING AND PRAYER. IT HAS BEEN WRITTEN THAT DURING THE DAYS WHEN NEPHI THE SON OF HELAMAN TAUGHT THOSE ANCIENT AMERICANS THE WORD OF GOD, MEN WERE LED TO SALVATION. "THEY DID FAST AND PRAY OFT, AND DID WAX STRONGER AND STRONGER IN THEIR HUMILITY, AND FIRMER AND FIRMER IN THE FAITH OF CHRIST, UNTO THE FILLING THEIR SOULS WITH JOY AND CONSOLATION" (HELAMAN 3:35).

STEP NINE:
CHARITY

Charity is the pure love of Christ
and the great commandment by
which all people should live.

It has been said that "charity never faileth." It does not fail in any situation because true charity comes from Christ, and Christ never fails. As we draw close to him and act in our lives according to his will and example, we will possess this love for all people.

God's love for us is personified in the gift of his son, whose love is exemplified in the Atonement. Our love for God is personified in our efforts to keep his commandments to love others and not envy, covet, or show anger, which provoke multiple other sins. What a heaven on earth if everyone behaved toward everyone else with patience and appreciation!

SO IMPORTANT IS CHARITY—GOD'S

LOVE—THAT THE SCRIPTURES URGE

US TO PRAY FOR HELP IN DEVELOPING

THIS ABILITY WITH ALL ENERGY OF

HEART, YIELDING OUR HEART TO HIS.

OBEDIENCE

Obedience is our demonstration of
awareness of the goodness of God's
counsel to us for a successful life. He
has said that if we say we love him,
we prove it by doing what he says.

Obedience is righteousness.
Righteousness is the oil of our
lamps of preparation to meet
the Savior.

BLESSINGS COME THROUGH OBEDIENCE, BOTH AS

A GIFT AND AS A REWARD. THE SPIRIT ATTENDS

US AND GOVERNS THE BODY, AND GIVES US

POWER IN DEVELOPING THE SPIRIT WITHIN US.

THROUGH OBEDIENCE WE GAIN SELF-MASTERY.

SELF-MASTERY

Self-mastery is when *wanting* to

becomes a commitment to *doing*.

As a ten-year-old, I would come home from
school excited and ready to play. We lived on
a farm miles from the city and neighbors. My
friends were my horse, Blue, and my dog, Ted.
I'd hurry with my chores, ready to play, but
sometimes Dad would have an additional task
like pulling weeds. I didn't like it, and I'd think
about hiding, but I wanted to obey because I
knew my father loved me and I respected him.

JOSEPH SMITH HELPED PEOPLE UNDERSTAND HOW TO GROW SPIRITUALLY BY MASTERING SELF A LITTLE AT A TIME. HE EXPLAINED: "WHEN YOU CLIMB UP A LADDER, YOU MUST BEGIN AT THE BOTTOM, AND ASCEND STEP BY STEP, UNTIL YOU ARRIVE AT THE TOP; AND SO IT IS WITH THE PRINCIPLES OF THE GOSPEL— YOU MUST BEGIN WITH THE FIRST, AND GO ON UNTIL YOU LEARN ALL THE PRINCIPLES OF EXALTATION."

STEP TWELVE:

ENDURANCE

People who yearn for spirituality must
not only hearken to the teachings of
the gospel along the way, but must
endure to the end. This makes the
difference in sincere gospel growth.

Spirituality is the greatest quest of the soul. It requires us to overcome temptation and obtain victory over the flesh. Spirituality is being in tune with God. It is saying "Thy will, O Lord, be done, O Lord, not my will," because he knows what is best for us and sees the beginning from the end.

Spirituality results in ears that

hear, eyes that see, and hearts

that feel for the welfare of the

kingdom of God.

We believe that an individual spirit inhabiting the new human babe does so through the power of God. Each spirit has a turn on earth. It has been so since the creation of earth. That new little earthling then must be trained through its particular time frame and mission assignment in life.

As the babe is trained—the twig bent—so becomes the grown person. With agency he must choose to endure, to live by God's principles always, and to become the spiritually mature being worthy of living forever in the presence of God.

Two important perspectives in life are knowledge of the human body and knowledge of the eternal spirit. What brings physical fitness and what stimulates the growth of our eternal spirit are great facts to acquire.

The Lord's promise says that "whatever principle of intelligence we attain unto in this life, it will rise with us in the resurrection. And if a person gains more knowledge and intelligence in this life through his diligence and obedience than another, he will have so much the advantage in the world to come" (D&C 130:18–19).

A SPIRITUAL PERSON IS MASTER OF

SELF, IS SPIRIT–DIRECTED, AND HAS

COME TO A STATE OF RIGHTEOUSNESS

AND PURE, REWARDING HAPPINESS.

A gift of spirituality is answered
prayers. Pray always to understand
what you hear when God's servants
speak, and listen with the purpose of
your own spiritual growth in mind.

President Joseph F. Smith was valiant spiritually to the cause of Christ. He said, "Let the spirit of this gospel be so imbedded in my soul that though I go through poverty, through tribulation, through persecution, or to death, let me and my house serve God and keep his laws.

"However, the promise is that you shall be blessed through obedience. God will honor those who honor him, and will remember those who remember him. He will uphold and sustain all those who sustain truth and are faithful to it. God help us, therefore, to be faithful to the truth, now and forever."

ray before you read the scriptures. Develop eyes that see with the quickening of the Spirit as you study. You'll find answers to problems, secrets for happiness, gifts to teach others or to guide a child.

In the Old Testament we read:

"And God said, Let there be light:

and there was light." It was the

first of his creations and he saw

that it was *good*. Then he divided

the light from the darkness.

So should we.

Even though light passes through dark
pollution, it does not become polluted,
observed St. Augustine. So it is with the
eternal spirit, which is light, and the
human body, which is of the elements of
the world and goes back to earth itself.

It follows that we should fill our souls
with light, and strive to strengthen
the light within us.

How do we do this? A step at a time!

As one candle takes flame

from another, as the moon

reflects the sun, so we can

bask in the light of the Lord

and spread light rays beyond.

When you are strengthened spiritually, help others become converted to the twelve steps to spirituality. Then one day the flood of spiritual gifts that follows faith will make a difference to more and more of Heavenly Father's children.

Our family has had its share of problems. Striving for greater spiritual strength has helped us weather many storms. I like what Joseph Smith shared: "You will have all kinds of trials to pass through. And it is quite as necessary that you be tried as it was for Abraham and other men of God, and . . . God will feel after you, and he will take hold of you and wrench your very heart strings, and if you cannot stand it you will not be fit for an inheritance in the Celestial Kingdom of God."

In the Bible we read that God the Father *gave* his only Son begotten in the flesh (miraculously with Mary) so that everyone who would believe in him would ultimately have everlasting life (JOHN 3:16).

Jesus Christ was our necessary Redeemer. He accepted this assignment before this world was. Many of mankind have not been taught this truth. We are thankful to have been taught the true way to spirituality—it is through closeness to the Savior.

about the Author

Ed J. Pinegar has served as president of the
Missionary Training Center in Provo, Utah,
and as president of the England London South
Mission. He has been a member of the Aaronic
Priesthood Committee and of the Young Men
General Board. He and his wife, Patricia
Peterson Pinegar, are the parents of eight children.

ISBN 1-57345-828-7

50795

9 781573 458283

SKU 4024471 U.S. $7.95